A Childcare Provider's Guide to:
Home Childcare Business

Dealing with Bratty Kids and Clueless Parents

AuthorHouse™
1663 Liberty Drive
Bloomington, IN 47403
www.authorhouse.com
Phone: 1-800-839-8640

First published by AuthorHouse   07/26/2011

ISBN: 978-1-4634-2636-1 (sc)
ISBN: 978-1-4634-2635-4 (ebk)

Library of Congress Control Number: 2011910393

Printed in the United States of America

Dedication

I dedicate this book to my son Dana Sean Julius, my grandchildren Patrick and Aaliyah, my loving niece Ashley Rogers, and my loving second son Tony Robinson. Lastly, to all childcare providers of the world who have put up with spoiled, unruly children, and their clueless parents who refuse to believe that their kids are out of control.

Table of

Contents

Table of

Contents

Author's Notes

If you are a home childcare provider or just a parent seeking insight, you will definitely appreciate this book.

After many years of taking care of children, I have discovered that it is not always the child who needs guidance. Often, it is the parents who need help. Especially when it comes to recognizing how spoiled and out of control their children really are.

Most of the time, I have found that the child is not being given home training. In these instances, I believe that the parents need child rearing classes or at least someone older and more experienced to help guide them in raising their children.

In this book, I offer numerous examples of children acting out and parents who cannot control them. You will also find actual steps guiding you through a start up childcare business with examples of what I experienced when I first opened my doors.

Everyone has to start at the beginning, and when I started my childcare, I had to learn quickly that in order to become successful; I had to wear many different hats and possess many different personalities. Boy was I shocked as to exactly how many hats and personalities I had to have!

First, I had to be a good listener (that was a given), and then an accountant, a pastor, a guidance counselor, a teacher, a marriage mediator, a confidant, and lastly a disciplinarian.

If you are thinking of starting a childcare business and you do not possess any of these skills, then my advice to you is, think again.

Don't delude yourself into thinking that all you need is a love of children. This is definitely very important; however, you need to open your eyes. All these other personal aspects will play a larger role in your success. If you do not possess them, then you are in big trouble and in for a letdown.

In addition to what I have already stated, I had to learn how to interview parents, observe their children, make quick assessments, develop guidelines for non-paying parents, and construct a workable schedule that would be successful for both the children and me.

In the following pages, I will give you valuable tips on these topics, and you will read about the dos and don'ts when starting and operating a childcare business. You will receive my wisdom, experience, and insight in becoming a successful childcare provider. And I hope that after all is said and done, you maintain your sanity in the process.

In closing, there are several points to note. For all those childcare providers out there, remember that you are not alone. Every situation is different, but much of what you experience is universal. Believe it or not, eighty percent of the parents you come across can be actually managed. It's the other 20% that will make you question not only yourself, but what's even worse, second guess your reasoning for venturing into the unique world of childcare.

For the parents reading this, if you find that you are seeing yourself in these pages, make an effort to change. It doesn't always mean that you are a bad parent. It can only help you identify new avenues and resources for increasing your knowledge in child rearing.

Always remember, any child you consider bad is not all-bad. What parents do in the beginning makes that child who they are, and what they will become.

Note: *Please be aware that the names in this book have been changed in order to protect the dignity and privacy of others. For purposes of this book, I will refer to my childcare as "Tiny Tim's."*

You can learn many things from children. How much patience you have, for instance. ~

Franklin P. Jones

Things to Remember

The very first rule you should remember in dealing with difficult parents and children is that it requires not only knowledge of how to handle them, but more importantly knowledge of how to handle yourself. Remember, you may not be able to change the child or parent, but you can change the way you interact with them which will ultimately change the way they interact with you.

For the childcare provider, following these simple rules below will help you deal with certain childcare situations:

- You must always be an advocate for the children.

- Always keep an open mind. Children and parents will do the unexpected when the expected is planned.

- Remember, this is your business. Run it like one!

- Never give favors to parents. If you do favors for one, you must do favors for all. Parents do talk!

- If you have a home childcare, check out potential parents thoroughly before accepting them. Especially if you keep children at night. You never know who is coming into your home.

Disclaimer

This book will provide information vital to the childcare industry.

It is not the purpose of this book to reprint all the information that is available to authors and/or publishers, but instead to complement, simplify and supplement other texts. You are encouraged to read all the available material, and to learn as much as possible about the childcare industry.

Every effort has been made to make this manual as complete and as accurate as possible. However, this is not to be considered the "Bible" of childcare. Therefore, this text should be used only as a general guide and not as the ultimate source of information relating to the childcare industry. Keep in mind that each child is different and unique. There are some general patterns in children that are predictable and repeat. This book is designed to help the childcare provider deal with behavior that is considered problematic in the childcare industry.

The purpose of this manual is to educate and entertain. The author and the publisher have neither liability nor responsibility to any person or entity with respect to any loss or damage caused, or alleged to have been caused, directly or indirectly, by the information contained in this book.

In the United States today, there is a pervasive tendency to treat children as adults, and adults as children. The options of children are thus steadily expanded, while those of adults are progressively constricted. The result is unruly children and childish adults. ~

Thomas Szasz

Chapter 1
Starting a New Home Childcare

I have been thinking about venturing into the childcare business for a very long time (years in fact). What made me decide upon this business? First, I have a love for children. Secondly, I felt that my teaching skills could be better used for my own benefit. Giving children a head start in their journey towards learning could be my greatest accomplishment. Lastly, I was just fed up with the games of the corporate world. I would rather have total control over my life and finances than have it depend upon some small-minded manager that wants to take all of their frustration out on me.

Therefore, with this goal in mind, I quickly learned that in order to venture into this kind of business, it required a lot of research, training, and consistent dedication.

I knew that I loved kids, but I was clueless to think that this was all I needed, and unprepared as to how many hours it would take to really open my doors for business.

To give you a general understanding of what one must endure in starting a home childcare, the following is an outline of some key steps I took in my journey to be a childcare provider. I began by doing the following:

- **Wrote a business plan** (this should be done first and is a critical step). You can find a very good example of a business plan at this website: **http://www.bplans.com/day_care_business_pl an/executive_summary_fc.cfm**

- **Conducted a market research campaign within 20 miles in all directions of my home base.** This may entail phone calls to local childcares inquiring about pricing, schedules, meal services, child-staff ratios, and hour availability. You may get some pushback from calls you make, but the more information you can gather, the better it will assist you in creating your own plan.

- **Obtained CPR and Child First Aid certification.** You can get this through your local fire department, college campus, or the Red Cross organization.

- **Obtain the State's Child and Family Services certification.** Each state lists their contacts on the Internet.

- **Obtained certification from the State's food program.** Some states have a food program that will pay for the number of meals that you serve your children. It is beneficial for you to contact your local service.

- **Joined several State Professional Childcare Organizations.** This will help you keep up to date on the latest childcare guidelines and regulations. It is also a great resource to exchange ideas and share your personal experiences.

- **Obtained State and County business licenses.** Some states require that you only have a county license, where others require both. Contact your local municipality for verification.

- **Took 20 hours (this is yearly) of childcare classes.** You may do this online, at a local college, or through your childcare associations.

- **Wrote parents guideline manual for my perspective parents.** This book covered everything a parent should know about my childcare.

- **Developed parent enrollment forms.** You will need some necessary forms covering child enrollment information. These forms should include childcare vaccinations, medical history, doctor listing, parent contact information, fee agreements, and trip permission slips. I have listed a great website for free forms in Chapter 16.

- **Established a Priceline.** This came from my market research.

- **Created a website.** This is a great marketing tool.

- **Copyrighted my childcare name, documents, and website.** There are many childcare **providers** popping up. Make sure that your childcare is unique and not copied illegally.

- **Opened a separate email account.**

- **Printed business cards.**

- **Created and Distributed flyers and signs within a 10 mile radius in all directions.**

- **Opened a business bank account.** One key point is to keep your business finances separate from your home finances. This will make it much easier at tax time.

- **Obtained a Federal Tax Identification number.** If you want additional benefits at retail stores and online business associations, this is a must. You can apply for this number through the Internet.

- **Obtained an Employee Identification Number.** This can be obtained through the Internet.

- **Renovated an area in my home for children's play and classroom.** A standard rule is 30 square feet of indoor activity space per child. This will give you an idea of how many children you can accommodate.

- **Installed a business phone and fax.**

- **Ensured that all children's room had an up-to-date smoke and carbon monoxide detector.**

- **Obtained fire department inspection.** Call your local fire department. They will conduct this inspection for free and provide you with batteries for your smoke detectors.

- **Retained a law firm that would work on a pro-bono basis.** This was used for those potential parents that would not pay me (discussed in a later chapter).

- **Purchased age appropriate toys, books, and learning materials for the children I was to care for (discussed in a later chapter).**

- **Purchased a "Touch Computer" for my toddler pre-K program.**

- **Purchased kitchen and cleaning supplies.**

- **Purchased playground equipment that was state approved and age appropriate.**

- **Obtained a P.O. Box.**

- **Calculated the costs of my monthly operating expenses, and developed a budget against the projection of money I planned to earn for the first year.** The marketing analysis was a great help in this aspect.

- **Distributed business cards to local retail stores.**

- **Prepared an Emergency Evaluation Plan.** This included written instructions as to where the children will be in case of disaster.

- **Joined the National Childcare Fee Default Registry** (Discussed in later chapters)

- **Posted exit signs in designated rooms**

As you have read this list, you are probably saying to yourself, "Wow that was a lot!" In reality, it certainly was." Nonetheless, I knew that I wanted to be successful, and from my previous corporate experience, I knew it had to be done right in order to succeed. Therefore, I stress upon you again, if you are thinking about opening a childcare business, especially a "Home Childcare," then these steps are critical.

OK, let's move forward. I have now done all my research, completed my key steps (discussed previously) and I think I am ready to open my doors for business. NOT REALLY! From 80% of the "key steps" that were listed on the previous pages, I discovered that there were sub-steps, which also had to be completed before I could really start my business. I will discuss these sub-steps throughout the next chapters.

In closing, please remember that if you want to be successful in the childcare industry, do not "half step." Be thorough in everything you do. Your success depends upon how the parents view you as a professional childcare provider. Your professionalism and the organization of your facility or home will have a huge impact on the parent evaluating your childcare operation. After all, would you want to put your child in a daycare home or facility that appeared less than professional? I don't think so!

Above all else, run your business like a business. If you are opening a home childcare, this is even more important. A successful business owner does their homework first, even before opening their doors. Don't think that doing things half way will ultimately reap the rewards. Believe me they do not!

Chapter 2
Making Your Home Childcare Safe

For a home childcare, the appearance of your home is critical in obtaining potential parents. Neat, clean, and sanitary rooms are the best presentation that you will have, next to the children's play areas.

Some suggestions I can give you are:

- If you are in the habit of keeping clutter around your home, get rid of it. Parents like to see non-cluttered rooms. Open spaces are even more appealing. Remember, the more clutter, the more opportunities there are for children to get hurt by things.

- Rooms should be spotless. Free of dust, dirt, and odors. Remember, just because you like the scent of wildflowers doesn't mean that everyone will like it. Smelling a clean scent is always better. This is also a helpful point to remember if a child has any breathing problems that might be triggered by dust, dirt, and odors.

- If you have many "nick-knacks," put some of them away or at least make sure that they are free of dust.

- Make sure that your furniture does not block the children's play path. Meaning, if children play in an area you use for your family, make sure that the furniture is kid safe and that they will not hurt themselves if they trip over or fall against an object. Again, no clutter!

- Ensure that you have safety plugs in all the outlets and corner guards on all furniture that has square edges.

- Purchase only FDA approved toys. Some toys made overseas have high levels of formaldehyde. This chemical is used to dry paint quickly. It is also hazardous to your health if used in high levels, and can cause health issues for children that put these toys in their mouths. For more information, view this website: **http://shop.perkinelmer.com/content/Applicati onNotes/APP_FormaldehydeInToysUVVis.pdf**

- Wipe (sanitize) down all toys and furniture in the children's play area daily.

- Purchase toys that do not have sharp edges.

- Ensure that your kitchen area is clean and that you sanitize all countertops, tables, chairs, and kitchen appliances daily. If you really want to see how clean your kitchen is, call the department of sanitation, and ask them to come into your home and check your kitchen out. In most cases, they will do this free of charge.

- Ensure that your bathroom is cleaned and sanitized daily. It should be free of mold or the appearance of mold. Potty chairs should be emptied and sanitized after every usage.

- Install fire extinguishers in the kitchen and the children's playroom. Ensure that the fire extinguisher in the kitchen is both compliant for smoke and carbon monoxide.

- Install fire detectors in all rooms where the children will be present.

- Purchase a baby monitor. You will definitely need this to not only monitor babies, but to monitor your children when you are not in the room.

- Your front and back yard must be cleared of clutter. Your grass and hedges cut neatly. Remember, an outside appearance is just as important to a potential parent as the inside.

- Ensure that if you have playground equipment, the ground is filled in with rubber mulch.

Above all else, never forget that the first impression is always the best. Make sure your first impression reflects your professionalism and dedication to detail. It will go a long way with current and future parents. They will get a feel of how you are as a childcare provider by the way your home or facility is maintained.

Note: if you are seeking state childcare certification, they will provide you with additional requirements.

"Safety and security don't just happen; they are the result of collective consensus and public investment. We owe our children, the most vulnerable citizens in our society, a life free of violence and fear." ~

Nelson Mandela

A Childcare Provider's Guide to Home Childcare Business -
Dealing with Bratty Kids and Clueless Parents

Chapter 3
How Safe Are Your Children

The safety of the children in your care is your top priority. To help ensure that your home, facility, or equipment is safe and kid friendly, I would like to give you some additional tips on certain things to consider. It is my hope that giving you these tips will ultimately prevent potential dangers to your children and yourself.

Burns

Did you know that the kitchen is the number one area where children can be injured? It is always best when heating or cooking food to keep children out of the kitchen.

I have found that even toddlers learn early that they cannot go into the kitchen when food is being prepared. If you place this rule in effect early, your children will learn that this area is not for play.

To prevent injury, follow these steps:

- Keep hot foods and drinks away from the edge of counters.

- Do not place plates on tablecloths. Children can pull the tablecloth and all of the dishes will go with it.

- Do not drink hot liquids while holding children.

- Keep children away from the stove.

- Ensure that no food given to the children is too hot.

- Make sure that all cooking appliances are off during meal times while the children are in the kitchen eating.

In case of burns, cool the burn with cool water. Do not use ice and never use butter or Vaseline. Call 911 for professional evaluation of the burnt child.

Falls

During childcare operations, frequent falls among children from the age of 14 and under occur almost every day. It has been documented that over 2.5 million children are treated in hospital emergency rooms every year for fall related injuries.

These falls may occur when children climb chairs and tables, running around the room too fast, riding bikes, or just playing on playground equipment.

Most playground injuries occur with children under the age of five when they are playing on equipment designed for older children.

To prevent these types of injuries, follow these steps:

- Ensure that you are monitoring the children's play period at all times.

- Make sure that your playground equipment is age appropriate and if necessary, fill in the ground around the equipment with rubber mulch.

- When choosing playground equipment and toys for toddlers, make sure that you choose things that children can grip easily. The hands of this age group require smaller grips and their bodies require appropriately spaced objects.

- Install window locks. You would be surprised how easy a toddler can open and squeeze through a window that is no more than 4 inches tall.

- Keep furniture away from windows. This might encourage children to climb.

- Do not allow children to run on hardwood floors or slippery surfaces.

Guns

You may think this sub-topic does not belong in this book, but let me tell you that every two hours in the United States, someone's child is killed with a loaded gun.

If you are operating a home childcare and you have a gun within the home, then it is extremely important that you store it unloaded in a secure location and that the location is locked and cannot be accessed by children.

Poisoning

In a childcare home, medicines, household products, and even plants can lead to children being poisoned.

To prevent these instances, follow the rules below:

Medicines

- Use child-resistant covers on all food and cleaning products.

- Keep medicines in a locked cabinet or store on a higher shelf out of the reach of children.

- After using medicines and cleaning products, return them to their storage place immediately.

- Never take medicine in front of a child. This can give the child an impression that they can do this too.

- Never tell the child that taking medicine is like candy.

Household Cleaning Products

- Use only products with child resistant caps.

- Keep cleaning products in a locked cabinet or store on a higher shelf out of the reach of children.

- Never put household products into food or beverage containers.

Plants

- Record the names of all plants and which ones are poisonous.

- Keep all plants out of the reach of children. This includes any room that the children have access to.

- Teach children not to put plant parts into their mouths.

Lead

- Check all windowsills

- Walls

- Blinds for peeling or chipped paint.

Miscellaneous Items

Remember to secure any rugs in your home or facility, as children will trip over the edges. If you have any bookcases or furniture that children will find attractive for climbing, secure these structures to the wall with a child safety strap.

Chapter 4
Payment Methods for Parents

In the childcare business, if you are a privately owned, listed, registered, or licensed childcare provider, a good rule to follow is to make it easy for your parents to pay their bill. The easier it is for them, the better chance you will have in getting your money on time.

In larger daycare facilities, this is not necessarily a problem, since they have the money and equipment to accept other forms of payment, and they have a staff that only handles this part of the business. However, with home childcare operations, this part of the business can make you or break you.

To educate you in this regard, did you know that if you are a privately owned childcare, you too could setup these same methods that large childcare facilities use with little or no money and effort? It is not as hard as you think. Below is a description of some easy to use methods for receiving money from your parents.

Cash - Cash is always the most preferred method for the childcare provider, but, unbelievably, it is not always the easiest form of payment for your parents to pay their bill. In today's world, most people think it is unsafe to carry large amounts of money on their person.

Money Order – Money orders are the next best thing to cash. The down side is that unless you have a bank account to cash this type of currency, some retail stores will not accept this form of payment. Make sure that the money order is drawn from a legitimate company.

Below are other methods of payment which may exceed cash or money orders as an option. They are:

Check - Check is another form that can be a good method -- until it bounces. When this happens, you will have to incur bank fees (some ranging from 35 to 55 dollars a check), and if you have used these funds to pay your bills, you may be looking at a more severe situation in the end.

On the other hand, if you are satisfied with using only the above method, then you should put into your contract a clause for "bounced checks." This clause should cover "late fees" and "frequent fees" for situations that continue to occur.

PayPal - PayPal offers the ability to accept payment for services rendered. This is good, but what you need to know is that PayPal will charge you a transaction fee for every instance. This might not be a good idea if you are budgeting for every dollar you receive.

In addition, if you want to transfer money from PayPal to your bank, it may take up to four business days for that money to transfer.

Credit Card - It is very easy to setup an eCommerce account over the Internet. You can search for these companies, but be very careful. Mostly all of them have hidden fees associated with each credit card transaction. Some fees are higher than others. I personally recommend a company by the name of "Merchant Warehouse." Their website is **http://merchantwarehouse.com**

Their fees are very low and you can accept Visa, MasterCard, and American Express credit cards. You can also setup recurring billing. Once they have approved your parent's credit card, they will automatically deposit the funds into your bank account and send you an email notification.

Web - I personally use a web-based pay solution through "Minute Menu Kids." They allow you to enroll your parents into the system and they send your parent a confirmation email with a username and password. Once you initiate an invoice through their software, your parent will get an email notification and they will have the option to pay their bill. Once they have initiated this action, the funds will be automatically deducted from their bank account. You, on the other hand will be able to see all transactions through the software and therefore you will have an accurate way of budgeting all funds. You will also have the option of paying a $1.00 fee per transaction or having the parent pay the fee. You may contact Minute Menu Kids directly by going to their website, which is **www.minutemenukids.com**.

Bottom line! Have more than one form of payment option available to your parents. Whichever one you choose, always have a backup plan in case something goes wrong.

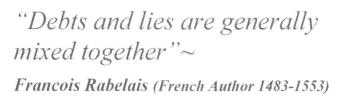

"*Debts and lies are generally mixed together*"~

Francois Rabelais *(French Author 1483-1553)*

Chapter 5

Bad Paying Parents - What to Do?

In our previous chapter, we discussed the different methods your parents can use when paying your childcare fees. In this chapter, we will discuss what you should do when these same parents do not want to pay you on time or leave your childcare not paying you at all.

If you have ever been in the childcare business for any length of time, or you are thinking about starting one, then you should know that there are some parents who feel that you work for free, and that you are not entitled to your paycheck on a timely basis.

When dealing with these types of parents, I have learned that some may regard you more like a servant, rather than a professional who will have a great influence on their child's future behavior and education. On the other hand, they may think that looking at the number of children that you have in your childcare, you are making enough money that you can afford to be generous, and therefore by-pass the due date of their payment.

Whatever their reason or abstract thinking, these parents should understand that this is a business, and not a charity. After all, would they go to the grocery store, place food in their cart, and then tell the cashier that they will pay them later? I think not! Payment is due upon delivery or in the case of a childcare, before service is given.

Don't they realize that if they do not have a reliable childcare provider, they will probably have to deal with some inconveniences of their own? Some of these might include, but not limited to:

1. They will have to stay at home to search for someone who can watch their child.

2. They may miss one, two or more days of work trying to find someone. In many of these instances, their employer will probably not pay for this time off or they may have to use their vacation time.

3. They need someone quickly, so they feel pressured to settle for anyone.

4. They have to deal with the consequences of the child's adjustment period. Moving children from one-day care to another can be difficult for a child.

In any case, they are losing both time and money, not to mention the adjustment of their child. So, why does it not make more sense just to pay on time the childcare provider that they currently have?

In addition to this, I have heard all kinds of hard-luck stories from these parents. Do not let them fool you, just like them; you need to show that your financial needs are just as important.

Below are some of the stories that I have heard:

- My car was repossessed and I have to pay the entire late fee before I can get it back. So, can I pay you next week?

- My electricity was cut off, and I must pay the bill with a security deposit. Can I give you a post-dated check?

  Note: If you go with this, it means that you are not going to be paid for at least one to two weeks, depending upon their timeframe. Moreover, believe me, there is no guarantee that the check will not bounce once it hits your bank account.

- My air conditioning went down and I have to pay a technician immediately, so can I pay you at the end of the week?

- My child support check did not come.

- My company's paycheck is late.

- I thought I had enough money in my checking account, but I do not. Can you wait until the end of the month when I am paid again?

- I got a final notice from my mortgage company and I have to get it caught up. Can I pay you installments of half pay for a month? I will make it up no later than the following month.

- My car broke down and I must get it repaired. It is the only car I have. It will cost me over $1,000.00 and I just do not have your payment

right now (no mention as to when they will
have it).

- Because I have other financial responsibilities, I
cannot buy food. Can you wait another week
for your payment?

- I just started a new job and I will not be paid until
two weeks.

- **This is a good one!** They do not mention at all
why they are not paying on the day it is due.
They pick up their child on that Friday without a
word and subsequently that following Monday
bring their child in to you without a word of
explanation or payment.

Believe me; the list goes on-and-on. Over these
years, I have learned to close my ears and heart to all of
this nonsense. The best way to get these parents from
exploiting your sympathy is above all else, do not listen,
and if you do go along with them, then you are expected
to do the same for all of your parents.

I admit, some hard luck stories are convincing, but
you as a business owner cannot continually give in to
these type of favors.

I have found, first and foremost that you run your
home childcare like a business. That means when your
payment is due, you have every right to expect it
on time.

Many parents have their priorities in the wrong
order. They feel that paying their childcare provider

comes last on their list, when in actuality it should come toward the top of their list. They should remember that if they do not have anyone to watch their child, they could not work. Moreover, if they cannot work, they cannot collect a check to pay for their basic living expenses.

First, to avoid these situations, most home childcares include in their contract a clause that states "payment is due on the Friday before childcare begins on the following Monday". An additional statement might follow warning that, "if this fee is not paid on time, then Monday will include a late fee of a specified amount."

My advice to you is to make the late fee large enough to deter any future late payments.

Secondly, when a parent starts to give you their hard luck story, start telling them how hard it is for you to keep the electricity on in your home, and if you do not get your payments on time, you don't know how you can pay your own bills. A statement from you might say, "I certainly have sympathy for you, and I can definitely relate to your situation. Every month I worry that I will not have enough money to meet my own obligations."

This counter-complaint tactic will in most cases, make those parents realize that you are not rich, and that you need your paycheck just as much as they need theirs.

Now, let us discuss what you should do when a parent removes their child from your care owing you back childcare fees.

In these instances, you should have a clause in your contract that deals specifically with this issue.

In my research, I have found a website that reports parents who pay late or leave while still owing fees. The website is entitled "The National Childcare Fee Default Registry," and their Internet address is **http://childcaredefaultregistry.com.**

As a member of this website, you get access to a report that lists all parents in your area who have delinquent fees. This report is very beneficial when you are considering accepting new parents. After all, would you want to accept a parent that left a previous childcare owing fees?

They also give you access to their lawyer (free of charge), who will send the parent a letter demanding payment. And if payment is not made, they will report that parent to all three credit agencies.

This website is strictly for childcare providers, and the public will not be permitted to view the reports. Once the parent has paid the childcare fee, only then will their information be removed from the website.

Conclusion:

1. Don't do favors when parents come to you with hard luck stories. In most cases, it is obvious that they are putting you last on their payment list.

2. Run your business like a business.

3. Have in the contract a clause that states late fee guidelines.

4. Bring your own sad story to the table when parents start giving you theirs.

5. Do not keep children of parents who are more than two days late on a consistent basis. You can be without two days' pay, but keeping children for a week without pay is not financially advisable.

6. Join the "National Childcare Fee Default Registry" website.

Communication is the real work of leadership. ~

Nitin Nohria

Chapter 6

Communicating with My First Parent

Now that I had completed all of the necessary steps for my business, I was ready to open my doors as a new childcare provider in the neighborhood. Let me tell you that I was so excited. Every day I waited for the phone to ring or my email account to blow up with new parents looking for childcare.

Well, not to disillusion you, but it took several months for my business name to get out there in the world. Therefore, my advice to you is, be patient and definitely have enough money stashed away to take care of your bills for at least a six month period. Not to say that it will take you this long, but you should always prepare for the worst.

Finally, the day came when my phone started to ring. Mind you, my experience in interviewing parents over the phone and giving them information was very limited at that time and I have to admit that as I look back, I made many mistakes. Just how many? I will outline them for you in the following paragraphs.

In addition, whenever there is a lesson to learn from my situations, I will refer to them as "**Red Flags**." These red flags will help you stop, think, and warn you against making the same mistake.

My first situation was as follows:

Parent Wanted Quick Childcare

I talked to a parent named Sally, who had a two-year-old named Jason. Sally had called me and was looking for a daycare for her son. She seemed in a hurry to find someone. Our conversation went like this:

Phone Call:	Hello, Tiny Tims, may I help you?
Caller:	Yes, do you have an opening for a 2 year old?
Me:	Yes, I do.
Caller:	How much do you charge?
Me:	I gave her my weekly rate (decided upon by my marketing analysis).
Caller:	OK, how soon can he start and do I need to fill out any paperwork?

Ok gang let us stop right here for a minute! This is a "Red Flag" that I did not see coming at the time. Although I did get the impression that this parent was in a hurry to get her son into childcare, I should have stopped and asked myself, why? I should have asked more questions, like "Has your child ever been in daycare before and if so, why did you remove him?"

This line of questioning would have given me additional information on the child and parent's previous association with other childcare providers.

In addition, I could have asked specifically what the name of the childcare provider was so I could check on the history. This would have given me additional information in making a decision whether to accept this parent and her child.

Remember, you do not have to accept every parent right away. You can always take their information and tell them that you will check your availability and call them back. This will give you more time to check out their story and to evaluate your own feelings about the conversation.

On the other hand, if the parent had said "no" to the previous childcare inquiry, I should have expressed my concern and stated to the parent, "I feel that you are in a hurry for childcare, am I mistaken?" Again, this would have opened up a conversation for the parent to elaborate on the reason why she was in a hurry.

Bottom line, the more you can get the parent to talk over the phone, the more you will learn about their situation and the child's background.

Let's continue with the conversation.

Me:	Well, first could I get your name please.
Caller:	Oh yeah! My name is Sally and my son's name is Jason.
Me:	Ok, but before I can accept him, I need to meet with you and your son. I'm sure that you would like to see my home and inspect the children's play areas first, right?

Note: Never meet with the parents without the child. You need to evaluate both the interaction between the parent and how they handle the child in a different environment. It also gives you a heads-up on the child's behavior. After all, an uncontrollable child will only make your day a living hell!

Caller:	Sure. How soon can we meet? Would today be OK?
Me:	No problem. How about 3:00 p.m.?
Caller:	That sounds great. I will see you then.
Me:	Thank you. See you later

There is that "Red Flag" again. What did I do wrong? I did not get her phone number, or her last name. This information would have been helpful if I had to call her either to remind her about the appointment or to cancel the appointment, or to begin checking her history with another childcare.

What happened at the end of all this? Well, I waited for this parent to show up. She never called and since I had not taken her contact information, there was no way for me to contact her.

Another "Red Flag"! The parent did not ask me any specific questions about my childcare. I would expect a parent to at least ask about my certifications, my background in childcare, how many children do I care for, or do I have a pre-k program. This parent did not ask me anything. She was only interested in how much money I charged.

Lesson learned. When screening parents on the phone, you have as much right to ask questions as they do. Below are some "inquiry questions" that you might consider:

1. Has your child been in daycare previously?

2. Is this your first child? Asking this question will give you a hint of how much you may have to train first-time parents. We will discuss this topic in a later chapter.

3. Will you be the only parent enrolling the child? This will give you some insight whether you are dealing with one parent, two, or other guardians.

   Note: In a home childcare, you should be aware of how many people will have access to your home.

4. Are you on CCMS (Child Care Management Services) or are you getting other state assistance?

    Note: This group is a state run agency that assists low-income parents with paying childcare fees. Each state has a similar program. Answering yes to this question means that the state will pay you a portion of the childcare expense. This guarantees that your childcare payments will always be on time.

5. What will be the time that you will drop your child off in the morning, and pick your child up in the evening? If you are a home childcare provider, this question is very important. Especially if you contract according to drop-off and pick-up times.

    Note: *Some parents, especially those working 12-14 hour job shifts may interfere with your personal time obligations. This question helps clarify this point before you meet with them face-to-face.*

    In addition, I have found that some parents think that they can leave their child with you more than 16 hours a day, five days a week. For a home childcare provider, you might as well say that you are raising their child, since they are with you more than they are with their own parent(s).

6. Does the child have any special needs? If you are not certified to take care of special need children, then again, this question is important. Some parents will not tell you this information over the phone. It is better to clarify this now, rather than wait until they show up at your door and be surprised.

7. How soon do you need childcare? If you are like me, I need time to prepare for a new child. I like to have at least a week to make sure that I have everything available for the new arrival.

These are only a few questions that you should consider asking over the phone. Once you have met with the parent and child, there are a whole other set of questions and statements that you can ask.

Once you have met with the parent(s) face-to-face, you should have a list of questions written out in front of you. This helps you stay on track and will ultimately, during the conversation answer many questions for both you and the parent.

These questions should come from your written childcare procedures discussed in Chapter 1.

Chapter 7

Face-to-Face
Parent Meeting

In the previous chapter, we discussed my first phone conversation with a potential parent, which subsequently resulted in arranging a face-to-face meeting (against my better judgment). Face to face meetings will provide you with a wealth of information. You should always follow up your telephone interview with a face to face meeting. And never see the parent without the child. Observing the parent interaction with the child will give you valuable insight as to the home environment.

Combined with the "Red Flags" that were present, I should have dismissed this parent right away, but as you recall this was my very first parent and I was really excited to at last have a potential child in my care.

Therefore, against all inward feelings, I arranged to meet with the parent at 3:00 p.m. that same day. Well, on the following pages, you will read what happens.

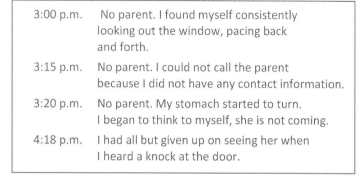

3:00 p.m.	No parent. I found myself consistently looking out the window, pacing back and forth.
3:15 p.m.	No parent. I could not call the parent because I did not have any contact information.
3:20 p.m.	No parent. My stomach started to turn. I began to think to myself, she is not coming.
4:18 p.m.	I had all but given up on seeing her when I heard a knock at the door.

Opening the door, I am facing a young woman, maybe between the age of 20 and 25. She has in her arms a small boy with a pacifier in his mouth, and a bottle in his hand.

I welcome them in. Mind you, she gives me no apology for being so late. (Here is that red flag again). When I mentioned that I thought our appointment was at 3:00 p.m. knowing perfectly well that it was, she casually stated that she had to take care of things around her house and just left out late. Big red flag, folks! Couldn't she have at least called me if she knew she was going to be late? It was obvious to me that if she did not want to call me, would she feel the same about paying me on time or paying me at all.

She introduced herself as Sally Smith and her son Jason. She said Jason was two years old. I proceeded to show her around my home and I noticed that she was still carrying Jason, so I suggested that she put him down and assured her that he could not be harmed on anything in the room.

Now why did I say that? The moment she placed Jason down, he immediately started to cry and threw his bottle down on my nice clean carpet, spilling milk all over. Trying to maintain calm, I stated, "No problem, I can take care of that." However, just five minutes in my home, I already began to look at this kid with some deep inward feeling of concern.

He immediately puts his hands up, indicating to his mother that he wanted her to pick him up again. The mother, in turn, with a very low calm voice says, "Now son, don't do that. Mommy will pick you back up shortly."

Oh No! Jason was not going to take that answer or her tone of voice. He immediately started to cry. Moreover, he got louder and louder, and louder, until he finally threw himself down on the floor and started to scream at the top of his lungs. Naturally, I no longer could think, talk, or even hear what the mother was saying to me. The mother on the other hand, seemed to totally ignore his behavior. It didn't seem to bother her at all.

Can you imagine what was going through my mind now? One thing was, why is she allowing him to act in this fashion and why isn't she being more forceful with him in order to correct his behavior?

She finally gave in and picked him up, which immediately stopped his crying. Ok, I am thinking to myself that this child is really spoiled. Looking at his angelic face, I know he is thinking to himself that he has won this battle. I am thinking on the other hand that this is not his first victory.

So, what am I thinking now? I am thinking how in the heck I am going to keep this kid. If his mother cannot control him, then how can I?

We now proceed to the children's playroom. When Jason sees all the toys, he naturally wants to get down from his mother's tight grip.

Once down on the floor, this little darling runs to the toy box and begins throwing all the toys out onto the floor. As I observe his behavior and the reaction of his mother, I am having those second thoughts again about him and what's even worse, getting into this industry. However, once I settle myself down, I think maybe he is just acting like this because his mother is here. Maybe I can correct his behavior on my own. All the while, I am still trying very hard to compose myself and keep from correcting this kid's behavior in front of his mother. I also wanted to push these red flags back into my mind because this was my first client and I want to make a good impression. Did I say that I wanted to make a good impression? What about the parent and her child?

Wrong, folks! You, as a childcare provider must remember that it is a two-way street. Yes, you must make a good impression, but on the other hand, the parent should try to do the same (if they can). The worst thing in the world is to have your child throw tantrums in front of someone that will be responsible for him or her more than 10 hours a day.

Fifteen minutes had now gone by and even through all of this, it felt like an eternity. I continued to struggle demonstrating my ability to handle Jason and go over my qualifications with his mother.

Jason, on the other hand is not cooperating at all. He even picks up a block and throws it, hitting me in my face. Oh, what a big red flag that should have been. I am thinking this kid is going to be a nightmare. What is even worse, his mother did not say a thing, not a word. Not a syllable, NOTHING!

It is obvious to me now that the mother is definitely over-spoiling this kid and is not disciplining him at home. It is also obvious that at home he is probably permitted to have tantrums, fits, and do pretty much whatever he wants without too much adult correction.

Another observation that I made was that he was two-years old and still had a bottle. What was up with that? Sippy-cup at his age, yes, that is appropriate. Bottle, I don't think so. He also had a pacifier in his mouth. Most pediatricians and speech experts recommend that a child stop taking a pacifier between 6 and 12 months. Any longer than this might affect their speech development.

OK, at the end of the interview the mother told me how impressed she was with my childcare and me. What a surprise, considering I barely got a chance to talk between all the drama that Jason was giving us.

She wanted Jason to start the following Monday. I felt at this point like throwing up. However, I said to myself again, this is my first client and I do need the money. I cannot turn them down, can I?

Note: If this happened to you, the answer is yes. You can certainly turn them down. I have learned that there is always a tactful way of refusing uncontrollable children and their non-attendant parents. The answer is being honest is the best approach. State exactly your feelings and concerns in keeping their child. This works better than making up excuses.

Bottom line – Did I accept this child with both his behavior and his mother's lack of discipline? I am sad to say, yes I did. However, after three weeks, I informed the parent that I could no longer keep him because of his uncontrollable behavior.

My decision was not totally based upon the child, but I later found out that the parent was as big a problem as her offspring.

She continually picked him up late. She rarely paid on time, and then refused to pay late fees. She always wanted to bring his special foods to eat, even though in the interview I specified that parents could not bring special foods, because the foods I served were in accordance with state inspections. Overall, she had generally become an irritant to both my childcare employees and me.

What did I learn from this first experience?

- The first meeting is extremely important. If you are not feeling good about either the parent or the child, then do not accept them. Always follow your first instincts.

- Sit down with the parent before they leave and go over your observations and concerns. Stress upon the parent that you want to build a partnership with them. Make it clear that you will not tolerate behavior that is abusive or uncontrollable. Get the parent's buy-in. Tell the parent to think about it for a few days and if they still want you as their childcare provider, then give you a call. This lets the parent know that you are not desperate for their business and you want to make sure that the parent totally thinks twice about your guidelines and discipline standards.

  Note: Oftentimes when you have a situation similar to the above, some parents will not come back because they know that their lenient methods at home will not work in yours. Thank goodness for that!

- Run a background check before you accept them as a client. You are inviting this person(s) into your home. You do not know who they are or what their intentions might be. The National Childcare Fee Default Registry reports parents who have defaulted on their childcare payments or who have a bad history associated with childcare facilities and childcare homes. Their website is:

http://childcaredefaultregistry.com

Conclusion:

- Follow your own instincts

- Observe the interaction between the parent and child

- Do a background check

- Listen carefully to the parent to pick up past history

- If necessary, prepare a question form to remind you of what questions to ask

- Take notes on what the parent has told you

We worry about what a child will become tomorrow, yet we forget that he is someone today. ~

Stacia Tauscher

Chapter 8

What Defines a Bratty Kid?

No child is born a brat, but they can be prone to bratty behavior if the parents do not put a stop to it early in that child's life. Even my kids had regressed into brats periodically when they were young. Nevertheless, staying consistent with what I expected from my kids allowed me to reel them back in to reality. My reality!

For those parents who are unsure if their child is a brat, here are ten signs to look for:

1. They resort to crying or yelling when they want something they cannot have, even to the point of falling out on the floor. They may even hold their breath or turn a shade of blue.

   Note: Don't worry about your child holding their breath. There has never been a case were a child dies from this.

2. They constantly throw tantrums or even hit and bite you when you punish them.

3. They hit or bite other children when they cannot get their way.

4. They ignore you when you give them a command.

5. They refuse to share with other children on a consistent basis or take toys away from other children.

6. They are show-offs and are constantly trying to be the center of attention. With this point, there may be a lack of attention at home.

7. They always want whatever anyone else has. Once they have it, they want something new.

8. They have crying spells, which mean they cry for no apparent reason.

9. They refuse to go to bed or take naps. Cry continuously until you come and get them.

10. They say "No" to you or refuse to follow your direction when you give them a command.

If your kids exhibit any or all of these behaviors, they might be brats. Please do not fret because there is hope for their bratty behavior and guess what? It starts with the parent!

Here are a few tips from my personal experience that will help curb brattiness:

- **Firmly discipline children when they show disrespect** – It is important to teach the child that disrespect will not be tolerated. They should be punished immediately and firmly when they disrespect you or other adults. Being punished might involve time-out, firm voice command, or even removal of a favorite toy. In some cultures, a small slap on the hand will usually do the trick.

Note: Some parents have told me that I have their permission to slap their child's hands. **Caution!** *If Child and Family Services has certified you, this is not a practice or option that I recommend. It could result in the removal of your license and certification.*

- **Develop consistent routines** – Children desire order in their lives even when they do not want it. They look to their parents and childcare provider to establish that order. Parents must set strict schedules for bedtime, homework, etc. and most of all, stick to the schedule. When the parents follow the childcare provider's schedule, it makes it easier for all concerned.

- **Teach them to be grateful and humble** – Brattiness is a symptom of selfishness. When kids learn the importance of serving others, they are more likely to be thankful for the things they have and understand that the world does not revolve around them.

- **Resist the urge to indulge their every whim** – As parents and childcare providers, we want to give our children nice things, but really people, does your 8 year old really need an iPhone? Don't buy them everything they want. Make them earn some things. This will teach them that rewards are earned, not given. With toddlers, teaching them early will have rewards later on. When they pick up their toys, reward them with a sticker or praise them. In addition, please everyone, remember, food is not a reward and should never be used as such. Example being, "Now Joey, if you act nice, we will go and get you an ice cream."

- **Spend quality time with your children** – Sometimes bratty behavior is a cry for attention. Show your child that they are important by giving them your time. Childcare providers should arrange some one-on-one time with each child. This helps tighten the bond between you and the child. It also gives the child a sense of feeling special because of your individual attention.

- **Compliment your child when he/she does the right thing** – Praise works wonders with children. Make sure the praise is sincere. Children know when they hear a patronizing tone of voice. Most importantly, you and the parent must be consistent with the child. It does not work if you as the childcare provider are doing the right things with the child and the parents are undermining your work when the child is at home. Discuss these matters with the parent and let them know how important these behaviors are for the child's social development. This also applies with the child's education (further discussed in a later chapter).

If you apply these suggestions, your brats will in most cases become more manageable and eventually you will see a reduction of bad behavior.

Your children need your presence more than your presents. ~
Jesse Jackson

Chapter 9
What to do With an Unruly Child

In this chapter, we will discuss the differences between an unruly child and a child that is just acting their age.

Many parents who seek childcare may be under the illusion that their little one is the perfect angel and can do little harm to their selves or others. Especially if this is their first child. Some new parents feel that the sun rises and sets on their little angelic being, and that in spite of what outsiders see, their child can do little or no harm.

Although you may think that very few parents feel this way, in my experience, I come across more than a few that go with this concept and take it way beyond the human imagination.

Unruly children act this way primarily due to some parents being too lenient at home. In other words, they let their child run wild. They do not set boundaries, and if they do, they surely do not enforce them on a consistent basis. You may ask yourself how this affects the potential childcare provider.

Well to put it bluntly, it makes a nightmare in hell look pretty good in comparison.

So, what can a childcare provider do, or be allowed to do in the case of having to care for a child that will not mind, will not stay still, disrupts other children, and ultimately will not respect an adult's authority?

Well, there are several things that you might do to make your life easier.

1. In your parent by-laws, place several clauses in it that deal with child discipline. Example: 1) you will verbally correct the child on the first instance, 2) on the second instance, you will reiterate your previous verbal warning, and 3) on the third instance, you will place the child in time out according to their age.

    > 1 year of age = 1 minute of timeout
    >
    > 2 years of age = 2 minutes of timeout, etc.

2. If the above does not work, then talk to the parent.

3. If after a reasonable period (normally within 1 month) the child has not stopped the behavior, then firmly tell the parent that if their behavior continues, you will be forced to withdraw the child from your childcare.

4. Make good your promise to the parent. Do not back down for any reason.

Remember first that this child is uncontrollable and you cannot sacrifice the well-being of your other children to correct the bad parenting that this child is receiving at home. Nor can you by yourself correct this behavior without the full cooperation of the parent. It is obvious that these parent(s) cannot control their child or they choose not to. This is their problem, not yours.

Remove the child from your childcare before it gets to this point.

My next suggestion is:

- **Turn a negative situation into a positive one** - If the child is doing something wrong, example being, pulling out all the other children's clothes from their cubbies, then instruct the child to pick up all the clothes and put them back into their proper place. Explain to the child that the other children's clothes do not get touched. If the child is not old enough to understand this statement, in a clear voice, look the child in the eye and firmly say "No," pointing to the item of concern.

- **Diffuse the situation** – If a child is showing signs of defiance or not minding you (example: saying NO to you), first correct the behavior by saying something like "you do not say no to me." Then you repeat the instruction again to the child. The next time you give the child a command and they follow your direction, without saying "No," give them praise and hugs.

- **Always Act Quickly** – Toddlers especially have short memories, so depriving them of a cookie after dinner because of an incident at breakfast pretty much ensures that they will not link the misdeed with its consequences. So, make sure you discipline them right after the infraction.

Conclusion:

- Always correct the child's behavior at the time you see it happening. Children, especially toddlers have short memory.

- Remember to praise the child when they do something right.

- If the child is uncontrollable after a period of time, consider removing the child from your care.

- Limit time-out according to the child's age.

- Communicate with the parent(s) the behavior of the child on a regular basis.

- Document the behavior in your daily notes (discussed in a later chapter).

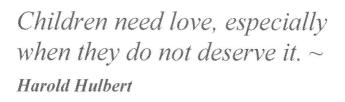

Children need love, especially when they do not deserve it. ~
Harold Hulbert

Chapter 10
Socialization of Bratty Children

What does socialization of a young child really mean? It can have many different meanings. One might mean to play appropriately with other children. On the other hand, it may mean to be at ease with other children and adults. Whatever the meaning you decide, just know that certain behavior is expected of our children when they interact with their peers and with adults.

Now I am sure as a childcare provider that you have come across children that are not comfortable or use to playing with other children. They are what we call "loners."

They come to you with many different behavioral problems. They hit, bite, scratch, cry constantly and generally they do not want to share or get along with the other children.

For a childcare provider, this can be a nightmare all by itself. What to do with this kid is the ultimate challenge.

In these instances, you need the full cooperation of the parents working with you to turn this kid around. If you cannot get that, then your success is non-existent and you might as well remove this child from your care.

Some of the things that I have tried relate back to "Chapter 9 – What to do With an Unruly Child." Nevertheless, in addition to my discipline procedures, there are a number of other things you can try that might turn this behavior around and make your day much more enjoyable.

I have tried the following methods with great success:

- Play more group games that allow the child to give toys or objects to other children. A good group game could be having all of the children sit in a circle and roll a ball to one another. This teaches team sharing.

- Have the children share in placing their toys back into the toy boxes. Then give them a group hug.

- When you see the toddler acting out by hitting, biting, or scratching, immediately get down on their level, (eye-to-eye contact) and with a firm voice, say "no." Then in a short sentence tell the child why this behavior is bad. Example: say, "no hitting."

- Once you have talked to the child that has caused the abuse, immediately go to the other child, making sure that the abusive child can see you, and give an extra amount of attention to that child. This action may make the abusive child know that their behavior was not acceptable.

- Try to anticipate when the child will hit and grab their hand before they make contact. This is probably the best method that works 90% of the time. It will reinforce to the child that bad behavior will not be tolerated.

Again, all of these methods may or may not work in your case, but I have found that if the parent continues the same methods, you will see a positive change in the behavioral aspects of a child and their interaction and socialization with others will improve.

In conclusion, let me reiterate again that if the parent will not discipline their child, then it is best for you not to accept this child into your care.

I have seen many children hitting, biting, and scratching their parents right in front of me and all I hear the parent saying, in a small voice, is, "honey, don't do that" or reach into their bag and give the child a cookie. As I have stated before, FOOD SHOULD NEVER BE USED FOR BAD BEHAVIOR.

"If we are to teach real peace in this world, and if we are to carry on a real war against war, we shall have to begin with the children." ~

Mohandas Ghandi

Chapter 11

The Education of Infants and Toddlers

What is Considered Early Learning for Infants and Toddlers?

Over the years, this has been one of the major debates among scholars, teachers, and the public. In this respect, I am writing from actual experience, and not from what people may say.

Children as young as 8 months old can start learning basic elementary skills. These skills can range from letters, numbers, shapes, and even words.

One of the most respected individuals in the field of toddler learning is Dr. Robert Titzer, Ph.D. Dr. Titzer's methods have engendered a wide variety of controversy, but in my viewpoint, his methods are right on the money.

Therefore, the first point I would like to make is that a child can start learning basic elementary skills from the age of 8 months right up to the time they enter kindergarten. During this period, the child is like a sponge. They will absorb any and everything around them. In actuality, their minds are much more receptive to new concepts than ours will ever be.

We have to take advantage of this critical and precious time in their lives before the outside world closes in on them. Naturally, this learning should start at home, but in 80% of today's world, this learning is actually conducted in various childcare environments. Why? Because in most cases, this is where the child will spend most of their time. Therefore, childcare providers should utilize this opportunity and know that this will be part of their daily responsibility.

How Do I Teach an Infant or Toddler?

When teaching this age child, you first must remember that children of this age learn by multiple methods and mediums. You must use sight, sound, touch, and hearing to connect to all of their learning senses.

Another tip would be to set aside a specific time of day that will be dedicated to this learning. At this age, most children learn best in the morning, immediately after breakfast. I have found that they are much more receptive to new techniques and their attention span is a lot longer.

For any child between this age group, placing them on the floor in front of a learning video can also be very beneficial. I am not talking about cartoons. I am actually referring to ABCs and number learning videos that show the object and then a related picture or theme. You can find these videos at your local "Teacher's Store." They are age appropriate and they normally display the age of the child who will benefit from this learning.

Another thing to remember is that children at this age have a very short attention span. Ensure that the video is no more than 15 to 20 minutes long. Any longer than that will distract the child and you will find yourself consistently saying "sit down" or "no, don't do that."

When teaching ABCs and numbers, only go over five items at a time (A-E or 1-5). Children at this age cannot remember the whole alphabet or one through 10. Once they have mastered the first five set of items, before you go on to the next set, you can reiterate the learning by playing a game that relates to these specific items. I find that the ""go-and-get" game works wonders. It helps reinforce what the child has learned and gives you verification that they are learning what you have taught them.

In the "go-and-get" game, a series of words, numbers, shapes, or ABCs is placed either on the floor or on a ledge surface. A child is asked to go and get your particular voice command. Example being, "Joe, go get the number 2 and give it to me." If the child were learning what you have taught them, they would immediately go get the number 2 from the surface or floor where you placed it.

After they have successfully completed the task, give them big praises, claps, and shouts! This will encourage them to do it repeatedly.

Frequency of Learning

When teaching infants and toddlers, you must maintain a consistent schedule. A good schedule might involve you doing certain things on certain days.

An example would be:	
Monday	ABCs (A - E)
Tuesday	Numbers 1 - 5)
Wednesday	Shapes (circle and square)
Thursday	Word Recognition
Friday	Free Play Day

These classes would again be performed in the morning. Afternoons and after lunch can be devoted to naps, book reading and crafts.

Making your own schedule and maintaining it on a daily basis is key to a young child's learning. If you are consistent, as a child gets older, they will know what day each lesson will be taught. You might even have pictures placed on a bulletin board that shows what day it is, and what lesson will be taught for that day. Children will surprise you. They notice everything.

Parents Who Do Not Follow Your Routine

Now that I have given you some insight on how to train toddlers, let me talk about the negative consequences of when parents do not work with you in the education of their child.

I remember when I took care of a one and a half year old boy. I took care of him for over a year and then his mother removed him from my care because she lost her job and could not afford the childcare fee. *Note: This happens frequently in today's economy.*

At the time of his removal from my care, he knew all of his ABCs; he could count to fifty and knew them by sight. He knew all of his colors and all of his basic shapes. This was a great accomplishment for a child his age.

Ultimately, eight months later, this parent came back and asked me to pick-up the care of her son, which I gladly accepted.

It was not even two days later that I discovered this child had totally forgotten 80% of what I had taught him. It was obvious to me that this parent did not spend any time going over his basic elementary skills. Subsequently, because eight months had passed and no reinforcement of lessons had been done, I was back at square one with this child.

This was very difficult, since now he was far behind my two year olds, and it was going to take extra effort on my part to bring him up to speed with the rest of the children.

When I mentioned this to the parent, she admitted that the people whom she let care for him placed him in front of a television all day long and did not put emphasis on any elementary learning. Naturally, she was sorry that she had ever taken him out of my care.

Personally, I did not blame the people who had taken care of him. I blamed the parent for not continuing or reinforcing what he had learned while attending my childcare.

In conclusion, as a childcare provider, please make learning a part of your daily routine. Do not think that you do not have a responsibility to teach your children. We as childcare providers have this duty and a lot more.

Don't just be a childcare provider, take it a step further, and be an effective teacher. Your parents will appreciate this effort and you will give your children a head start in their journey toward learning.

No symphony orchestra ever played music like a two-year-old laughing with a puppy. ~

Bern Williams

Chapter 12
Pets and Children

Unlike large childcare facilities, having a home childcare business you may have pets within your home. These pets, in some cases are your family members and they deserve just as much respect as the people who live with you.

In this regard, when you open your doors to a home childcare business, some parents, especially "new parents," feel a little bit apprehensive about letting their little one stay in a home that has one or more pets.

Dogs turn off some parents. Others are turned off by cats. It is up to you to assure the parent that your pets are safe, and that they pose no threat to their children.

I for one have pets (one dog and one cat). I recently had a parent come into my home for an interview and was very impressed with my environment. However, when I mentioned that I had pets, the mother quickly stated to me that she had a fear of animals.

I did not pry into the reason why she had this fear because bringing up old wounds definitely would not help the situation. Instead, I mentioned the following to help reassure the mother of her child's safety. I stated:

- That all my pets had up-to-date shots and were free of disease. I showed her the veterinarian's shot record and letter of authentication.

- That Child and Family Services had cleared my pets for my home childcare business.

- That according to the National Canine Association, my dog had a temperament that works well around children. I showed them the profile that I obtained from the Internet.

- That my dog did not shed, so therefore if her child had allergies, my dog would not affect them.

- That my cat had her claws removed, so she could not scratch the children.

- That my dog was sent to the groomers monthly, and washed by me in-between these times.

Once I had provided the necessary documents and discussed the previous key points, this issue was temporarily resolved.

I use the word "temporarily," because several weeks after I started caring for her child, she was consistently looking for signs of bites, scratches or the occasional sneeze from her child that would make her believe that my pets were to blame.

My advice to you is if you interview a parent that seems overly concerned with your pets, it is best for you to reconsider taking their child. I say this because in the next chapter I will go over necessary documentation that will save you many restless moments when dealing with these nervous parents.

Chapter 13
Home Childcare Documentation
What to Record on a Daily Basis

Now that we have covered how to start a home childcare business, and some of the children and parents that you will have to work with on a daily basis, it is now time to talk about what you should record in a daily diary on each of your children.

This last aspect is extremely important. It can be a legal document that can save you hours of dispute and is permissible in court for your defense.

Because you operate a home childcare, many parents will find all kinds of reasons to blame you for a variety of accidents. From scratches, bruises, stomachaches, and even common colds, some parents will swear that you did or did not do something to prevent it.

This is where your daily documentation will be a key factor in proving your innocence.

To reiterate my above comments, I would like to share with you several stories of parents that felt their child was being abused at my home.

For this first case, I will call the mother Joan and the little boy Peter.

At least twice a week, the child would come into my home in the morning with a scratch or some kind of bruise on his body. Twice he actually came in with a black eye, and immediately I asked the parent how he did this. I knew that he came into my childcare in the morning with these injuries because I would examine him every day (once in the morning and once before he was picked up). The latter was to ensure that he did not sustain any injury while he was under my care. Naturally, when I examined him in the morning in front of the parent, I did this discreetly, by looking him over when I took off his coat or sweater. Alternatively, on other occasions I'd examine him by me hugging him. After the parent left my home, I would examine him more thoroughly.

When I did find a bruise or scratch, I would immediately go to my computer, pull up his daily record, and make a notation. I would write on what day I found the bruise and where exactly it was located on his body and the time that I discovered it. As stated above, twice the child arrived in the morning with a black eye. I immediately asked the parent the question, "how did he do this?" thinking it might be child abuse (which if it was, I would immediately contact Child and Family Services to report it). I would then make a notation as to what the parent told me.

After several months of observing these injuries, the parent came to me and said, "How is he getting all these scratches and bruises here?" I immediately pulled out the last several months of notations and pointed out to the parent that I had asked them on several occasions when he arrived at my home, how did he get these bruises. I also informed the parent that every time I noticed a bruise or scratch on his body when he arrived at my home in the morning, I would make a notation of this instance.

Needless to say, the parent looked really surprised and apologized for accusing me of any wrongdoing. I also noticed that after this instance, the child did not come to me with a bruise for the next six months, which I notated as well. The parent did mention in-between this time that the child was really rough at home and that she was going to watch him more closely.

In this second case, I was caring for a little girl about two years old. The mother, whom I will call Tisha, was very paranoid about this child's care. From day one, she would imagine all sorts of things. On this particular instance, it was implied that because the child came down with a stomachache, that somehow the food that I was serving gave the child food poising.

The little girl always had a hefty appetite in that she would eat more than the other children and always ask for a second helping.

On this particular Friday, the father of the child came to pick her up. He mentioned that he was going to take her out to dinner, and I replied that I thought it was a nice thing to do. The following day, I get an email (notice here that the mother never called to talk to me) from the mother asking what she ate at my house the previous day. She stated that the child was throwing up and did not sleep at all that previous night.

I called the mother since I felt that this situation warranted a phone conversation. I stating that we did not have anything out of the ordinary and that she had eaten all of her meals, and did not show any signs of discomfort.

I asked if she had talked to the child's father, and she told me that she had not.

People, this goes to show you that any little thing that goes wrong with their child, you are the first person that parents look to.

In this instance, I immediately logged into the child's record and documented everything the mother was asking me. At the end of all this, the mother found out that the father had taken the child to eat at a restaurant, which served Asian food. This obviously did not agree with the child, since she had never eaten this type of food at her home or mine. Moreover, what did I immediately do when the mother told me this story? You are right. I documented the conclusion of this situation into the child's record.

To reiterate this again, the old saying "Cover your A_ _ "is definitely a must when you operate your own home childcare business. Follow your instincts if you have even a small hint of an action or statement coming back on you. Log the instance into the child's record immediately.

After all, you cannot afford to lose your license because of a paranoid parent.

The last example I would like to share was with a parent that blamed me for not changing their daughter's dirty diaper. She stated that when she got home, she had to change the diaper and that her daughter always had poop on her. To help her case, this parent had her two-year-old daughter spread her legs while she took a picture of the child's vagina and then sent it to me over the Internet. OVER THE INTERNET! What was she thinking?

I explained to the mother that according to state regulations, I change the children's diapers three times a day, and with her daughter, sometimes more, depending upon her bowel frequencies. I also explained to her that the last diaper change always occurred one hour before the parents picked up their child and if I detected them soiling their diaper, I would immediately change them.

It was obvious to me that when the child left my home, she was not soiled. However, on the way to the parent's home, this little darling would deposit a large poop, combined with a gas movement.

The mother, seeing that I was strong in my commitment to cleanliness, confessed that her daughter could have possibly done this on the way home.

I personally feel that this parent, from her past history with me was more than paranoid and just did not want to see or change her own daughter's dirty diaper.

Whatever the reason, again this is another example of parents blaming you for their shortfalls. This parent eventually apologized to me, but by then it had put a strain on our relationship, which ultimately I asked the parent to withdraw their child from my care.

These examples may seem out of the ordinary, but in actuality, they are not and I am sure that as a childcare provider, you could probably come up with examples of your own.

To help you in documenting these types of instances, on the following pages is an outline of what you should notate on each child by age:

Children 0 to 1 year

- Number of diaper changes per day.

- Any diaper rash.

- Number of ounces of milk the child drank (whether this is milk, formula or breast milk).

- How many naps the child took, what time, and how long they slept.

- Any observation as to motor skills (eye contact, body movements, or crying spells).

- Activities performed with the child, such as reading books or exercising body parts.

- Any other observations that you feel important.

- Parent's comments that seem out of the ordinary.

Children 1 year +

- Potty training activity (did they go to potty or not).

- What was eaten at mealtime and did the child eat all or some.

- What time did nap happen and how long did they sleep.

- Any observation as to motor skills (eye contact, body movements, or crying spells).

- Activities performed with the child, such as reading books or exercising body parts.

- Progress report on educational activities (ABCs, numbers, shapes, words, colors, etc.).

- Any other observations that you feel important.

- Parent's comments that seem out of the ordinary.

In many of the above instances, you may feel that documenting all of these instances can be very time consuming. You are right, but the end result always outweighs the means. After all, five minutes of documentation is much better than a long period in front of a child and family court.

Chapter 14

Legal Processes You Should Follow

In a childcare, there are many legal pit-falls that you may come across that will put you in an awkward and potentially dangerous situation.

One of these aspects may entail the separation or divorce of one of your children's parents. This can be a messy situation if you side with one parent over the other.

The first rule to remember in situations such as this is once the parent has informed you that they have separated or have divorced, have legal documents on hand that state this fact and who has custody and what that custody entails.

One example that I came across was as follows:

My first impression of this family was one of high respect and of a stable environment for the child. Over the course of one year, I learned that what is seen from the outside might not necessarily be what is seen from the inside.

Ultimately, as I listened to both the mother and father relay to me their marriage horror stories (Note:

not offering any opinion of my own), I learned that the marriage was indeed in turmoil.

This resulted in their separation. The mother, not wanting the father to have anything to do with the child, told me not to let him pick the child up from my childcare.

Now, let us stop for a moment! Do you remember those "red flags" that I talked about earlier in this book? Well, that red flag immediately showed its ugly head.

Because they both, at the beginning of our childcare contract had signed a "pick-up" agreement stating who had the authority to pick up their child; I had this document as my backup.

I immediately showed it to the mother and informed her that if I did not have a legal document outlining separation privilege that I had to go with what was signed and dated on our childcare contract.

The mother, not liking the situation said, "Well, you don't have to open the door and let him in. You can just call me and I will come over."

I responded to her stating, "I am sorry that you are going through such a terrible time, but again, I cannot accommodate you in that way. I definitely need a legal document stating that the father did not have any legal right to pick up his child from my care."

When I saw the father, I informed him of the same agreement.

To this day, I still take care of the child, and guess what? Legal documents were indeed brought to me stating that both parents had custody rights and that both parents had the right to pick-up their child from childcare.

What have we learned? If I had refused the father to pickup his child, he could have called the police, and I would have been charged with kidnapping and obstruction of justice against the father's rights.

Above all else, even though you think your parents are the sweetest people on earth follow the law and make sure that your contract supports the law for these instances.

Chapter 15

What to do When Parents Remove Their Child

For most home childcare provider's the consequences in losing a child may impact the reduction of financial security, not to mention the stress that you feel in trying to replace that child if you are depending upon maintaining a certain child quota.

In this chapter, we will discuss what happens when parents remove their child from your care. We will discuss how you should react and what steps you should take to execute a smooth departure.

Step 1 - Prepare for future removals of children

Always keep in mind that you will not be able to keep your children for any length of time. One negative factor in childcare you should know is that it is an up and down business. Based upon the parents' personal situation or attitude, they will remove their children from your care in "a blink of an eye."

Because of this, you must have a back-up plan. This plan might include a waiting list, periodic flyer distribution, price discounts, or newspaper advertisements. The point to this is, always keep your name out there, even when your child capacity is full.

Step 2 – Include a Departure Clause in your Parent's Guidebook

In chapter 1 we suggested that you write a parent's guideline manual. Within that manual, you should include a section on child departure. Most childcare operations require the parent to give a two-week notice when they want to remove their child. Once you receive this notice, you should do several things:

- Ask the parent why they are removing their child. Ask them specifically if it is anything that you have done that led to this action. There may be a number of reasons why the parent is doing this. It may be job related, marriage, financial, or some other personal reason that they do not want to discuss with you. However, you should try to get the parent to state if there was anything wrong with your care. These points will be critical in both a personal and legal aspect.

- Remind the parent of the two-week notice that they agreed upon and signed in your childcare by-laws and contract.

- Document in your notes everything that was said between you and the parent.

- Give the parent a release letter notating the date they gave you their notice, date of expected release, and a summary of the conversation outlining the reason for the removal. Have the parent sign the release letter. Give them a copy and you keep a copy for your records.

- Do not take this personally. Retain your composure and try to see this from the parent's point of view. Never show anger, no matter what the parent says. Say as little as possible. Getting into a long conversation or trying to change the parent's mind will only cause you to say something that you might regret. Be concerned, but not reactive.

Following the above steps will eliminate a lot of anxiety and stress. Both for your parents and yourself.

Chapter 16

Associations and References

The following list of associations and references will help you further your knowledge of childcare. I have found these organizations extremely helpful and vital to my daily operation. All of the below can be accessed through your local Internet search engine.

- Your State's Child and Family Services Organization

- National Association of Childcare Professionals (NACCP)
  http://www.naccp.org

- Dr. Robert Titzer, Ph.D – "Your Baby Can Read"
  http://www.yourbabycanread.com

- Sittercity Website
  http://www.sittercity.com

- Care.com
  http://www.care.com

- International Nanny Associations - Childcare Associations
  http://www.nanny.org/index_new.php

- The National Childcare Fee Default Registry
  http://childcaredefaultregistry.com

- U.S. Department of Education
  http://www.ed.gov/

- National Childcare Information Center
  http://www.csrees.usda.gov

- National Network for Childcare
  http://www.nncc.org

- Center for Childcare Workforce
  http://www.ccw.org

- The National Education Association
  www.answers.com/topic/national-education-association

- State local NutriService Food Program

- Minute Menu Kids Software
  http://www.minutemenukids.com

- Department of Child and Family Services (Free Childcare Forms)
  http://www.dss.louisiana.gov/index.cfm?md=p agebuilder&tmp=home&pid=183

- Employer Identification Number
  http://www.irs.gov/businesses/small/article/0, ,id=98350,00.html

- Tax Identification Number
http://www.irs.gov/individuals/article/0,,id=96 287,00.html

About the Author

A retired corporate operations executive with an additional 20 years of training experience, T.R's career always included the teaching and directing of educational environments for all ages.

A devoted Christian, T.R. taught in church environments, subjects ranging from elementary basics to computer science. In addition, T.R. spent many hours volunteering at local shelters for the betterment of those less fortunate.

T.R.'s philosophy to start a child's learning as early as possible proved to be the biggest success, since the majority of T.R.'s daycare children have far exceeded regular kindergarten pre-K curriculum.

T.R. was a single parent who raised her son on her own in the inner city of Chicago, Illinois. Her success and dedication to learning has been instilled in her son who now holds four degrees and a doctorate in law.

T.R. now resides in Arlington, Texas and is currently devoting herself to her church, her family, her community, and her childcare business.

To order a copy of this book, fill out the information below:

I would like to order a copy of:
A Childcare Provider's Guide to: Home Childcare Business Dealing with Bratty Kids and Clueless Parents

First Name			
Last Name			
Address:			
City:			
State:		Zip Code	
Phone No.:			

If ordering through our website, go to:
http://www.authorhouse.com

If you would like a mail delivery, please submit your payment to
Authorhouse
1663 Liberty Drive $12.95
Bloomington, IN 47403

If ordering by phone, please call: 1-800-839-8640. Please have your credit
card information available.

If contact and mailing information is the same as above, please check this box to right.	

Credit Card being used:	*Check box below*
Visa	
MasterCard	
AmericanExpress	

Name on Credit Card:	
Card Number:	
Expiration Date:	
Security Code (Found on back of card)	